"It's incredible what Rachel Madorsky has accomplished in this sweet, simple book. So pure and powerful. A balm for the inner child and the grown adult alike. Brilliant!"

"WOW. Absolute WOW. My heart was singing the entire time, and then I got to Chapter 15! This book is revolutionary and the right words to uplift us."

"This small book from Rachel Madorsky is the love letter your heart needs now. Maybe you're like me and you grew up with a lot of mixed messages about your value and merit. This book contains tips, exercises and kindnesses to undo all that and set you on the path to loving that person in your mirror."

"I freaking love this book so much. It is simple, subtle and powerful. I buy stacks of copies and give them out to everyone."

"This little pocket guide is like a soothing balm when you need the kind of words that hug your broken pieces back together. It's a beautiful reminder of how to be gentle with ourselves as we learn to nurture self-compassion and deepen self-love."

STACEY MORGENSTERN, international speaker, entrepreneur, master coach and co-founder of Health Coach Institute

"I am obsessed with this book. Most books and teachings on self-love are rooted in strategy. Things to DO to feel more love. Rachel has written a self-love book that is rooted in BEING, by practicing the deep, experiential and profoundly powerful unconditional love that changes us all. Few people on earth understand, practice and teach self-love the way Rachel does. Not only does this book offer beautiful and practical teachings on love, as you read, you can feel your understanding of real self-love grow. This book of simple practices is a powerful manifestation of real love, taught by a world-class master."

VANESSA BROERS, coach, speaker, author of *We Are One: How One Woman Reclaimed Her Identity Through Motherhood*

"Don't be fooled by the apparent simplicity of this little book. Within its pages, is a powerful, potentially life-changing message. Readers will be uplifted by the gentle nurturing words and the suggestions for cultivating self-love. If we all followed the wise practices contained in this book the world would undoubtedly be a better place!

TERRI PERLMAN-HALL, Psy.D., clinical psychologist

HOW TO LOVE YOURSELF

In Less Than a Week
& Also for the Rest of Your Life

 Rachel Madorsky, LCSW

Printed in the United States of America

Hardcover ISBN: 978-1-958714-12-6
Paperback ISBN: 978-1-958714-11-9
Ebook ISBN: 978-1-958714-13-3
Library of Congress Control Number: 2022942355)

CHICAGO · NEW YORK · PARIS · ROME

Muse Literary
3319 N. Cicero Avenue
Chicago IL 60641-9998

Dedication

*For every little girl who wanted more
and every woman who said yes to herself,
your love and joy are big enough to heal the world.*

Introduction

Self-love is a practice. It's a real and tangible skill you can learn. As you read the words on these pages I hope you will feel deeply loved and cared for. Sink in like a warm bath or gently dip a toe. There's no wrong way. Only love.

Chapter 1
Decide

Decide today is the day. You can say to yourself
in these words or your own:

Today is the day. I will love myself from now on.
It doesn't matter how much I do or do not
understand fully what that means or how to do it.
I'm in. I promise to learn, and I promise to enjoy
the learning. I love myself, no matter what from
now on.

Today is the day!

Chapter 2
Ask Yourself

Ask yourself: "What is one loving thing, no matter how small, that I could start doing today as a gentle reminder and expression of loving myself?

Many years ago when I finally decided I was going to love myself, even if I didn't know how yet, I started buying flowers at the grocery store. I'd put one beautiful flower in a vase on the nightstand next to my bed. This would be my own sweet reminder that I am loved … by me.

Chapter 3
Be Gentle

You are worthy and deserving of love and you don't have to work hard to earn it, get it, or prove it.

You're allowed to relax. Where can you let yourself off the hook? Where can you reduce the effort and release the pressure?

Busyness is a habit that keeps our love, pleasure, and freedom just out of reach. It's fun to be busy sometimes.

It's also fun to relax. Be gentle with yourself
and your time. You are the chooser of how you
experience your time.

It's Love o'clock!

time to relax!

Chapter 4
Personal Love Mantra

Create a mantra (or a few) that you can use daily. Repeat them until they become a love habit. For example:

- 💜 *I deeply and completely love and accept myself.*

- 💜 *I can feel love and joy filling every cell of my body and it feels amazing.*

- 💜 *I allow peace to flow from my heart and mind.*

- 💜 *I love you.*

* Note: the more often you repeat these words sincerely to yourself, the more authentically they will become a part of your life.

Here's the trick … when you say the words to yourself (they can be out loud or silent in your mind) practice slowing down and bringing the words, like a feeling and idea into your heart. This is key. Gently. bring. them. in.

If you find it hard to believe the words, that's okay. Love the part of yourself that finds it hard to believe and instead create a mantra that feels real. For example:

💜 *I am willing to love and accept myself.*

💜 *I am willing to feel worthy.*

💜 *I am willing to practice receiving good things on a regular basis.*

Practice bringing these ideas and feelings into your heart every day, whenever you can, whenever you think of it. It helps to write them in a journal and on post-it notes, and tape them to the bathroom mirror.

When you practice the mantras, do so with gentleness. There is no need to get anything right. It only matters that you be real. You don't have to pretend anything ever again, for anyone ever again. Loving yourself means letting you be you.

Chapter 5
Make a List

Make a list of things that you are tolerating and things that are not working. Draw a line down the page. Across from each item on your list write what you would prefer instead.

Looking at the list of what you would like instead, what action, no matter how big or small, can you take now to give yourself the things you prefer? This is your sacred to-do list. Let yourself enjoy doing the things and do them with love.

* For best results, write this exercise out on paper (writing may allow your creativity to flow easier than typing). For maximum effect, buy yourself a giant white board … whoa!! It feels good to see your thoughts and life get organized and loved on a big space with color dry erase markers!

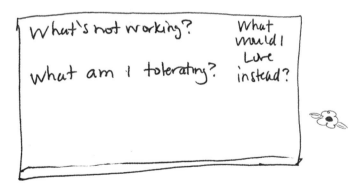

What's not working?   What would I Love instead?

what am I tolerating?

Chapter 6
The Love Inquiry

When in doubt about anything at all, slow down. Gently and sincerely ask yourself: What is the most loving thing I can do for myself right now? Listen for the answer. There will always be an answer. Do the thing.

Make a practice of asking this question frequently
and as needed, allowing yourself to listen to the
answer that arises. Practice giving yourself the gift
of tuning in, listening and saying yes to yourself.

Another healing question to ask is: What are the
most loving words I could say to myself right now?
Let the words reveal themselves to you. Say them,
write them, think them, give them to yourself.

Chapter 7
Forgive Yourself

Part of loving yourself is also forgiving yourself, for everything. This doesn't take away our responsibility (ability to respond). We can be responsible, fix our mistakes and apologize if we want to - all while totally and completely loving and forgiving ourselves.

Punishing yourself will never make it better. Only love, forgiveness and understanding will give you the peace of mind you crave.

Lean into a mantra that feels good. Here are some ideas:

- 💜 *I unconditionally love and accept myself.*
- 💜 *I love myself and easily let things go.*
- 💜 *I forgive myself for judging myself.*
- 💜 *I forgive myself for thinking I was wrong.*
- 💜 *I forgive myself for feeling so unforgiving.*
- 💜 *I am willing to forgive myself.*
- 💜 *I am willing to love myself.*
- 💜 *I am letting myself be free.*

Chapter 8
Practice Receiving

Loving ourselves means increasing our capacity to receive. There's nothing selfish about it.

The more you receive, the more you will teach yourself that it is safe to do so and that you are loved.

The more we receive the more we give naturally, from abundance, from the overflow, from our authentic self.

Be open to the compliments that come your way. Say thank you and **believe** the nice things that people say about you. Allow people to open doors for you, literally and figuratively, practice enjoying it. When in doubt ask yourself: "What would I, as a benevolent expert in receiving do?" Practice allowing yourself to love the love that comes your way.

Chapter 9
Make a New List

At the top of a page or on your white board, write: *I give myself everything I want, because I love myself.*

In two columns write down the things you would LOVE to give yourself on one side and on the other side write down the things you would love to let go of, release or delegate to someone else.

With a light-hearted touch, become a self-love strategist. What's that you may ask?

A self-love strategist is a person who, through self-love, helps themselves (and by doing so helps others), gives themselves everything they would give themselves if they were deeply and completely loving themselves, and lets go of and releases everything they would no longer be dealing with, doing, or tolerating, if they were deeply and completely loving themselves.

Like a magic wand, see yourself receiving the things you want (you will now be giving them to yourself) and see yourself poofing out of the way the things you no longer want your attention on.

The wand is you and the magic is love.

Chapter 10
Give Yourself Permission

You are your own fairy godmother, best friend and hero. Hug yourself (it's good for the oxytocin).

Be around people who love you, see you, lift you, energize, and appreciate you.

You don't want to go to that stuffy get together? Great! Don't go.

You want to start wearing dresses? Great! Do it.

Let yourself be fully you. This is your beautiful life. You don't owe anyone anything.

Chapter 11
Have Kind Thoughts

Our minds like to think and make meaning of things. We often think that things are about us. That's understandable. At the same time, what if nothing anyone ever did, or thought was about you. It's always about the other person – even when they think it's about you!

Practice having kind, compassionate and complimentary thoughts—especially about yourself.

Any time you notice a not nice thought, that's okay, good for you for being aware and noticing! And then replace it with something kinder. Practice kindness toward yourself in your thinking. You are worthy of kindness, always.

"Oh, that was dumb" can change to "Actually, you were in a hurry and life happens. You look really pretty today."

Chapter 12
Replacing Should
with Could

This one shift has the power to change everything. Practice with your thoughts as well as your spoken words. Change any should to could for yourself and others and see how it feels.

For example:

♥ I should go to the gym ➜ I **could** go to the gym.

♥ I should call so-and-so ➜ I **could** call so-and-so.

♥ I should be making more $$$ ➜ I **could** be making more $$$!

"Should" is infused with judgment, shame, and fear. "Could" is filled with freedom, acceptance and possibility.

Sometimes we think that pushing ourselves is the way to achieve the things we desire. We doubt that loving ourselves or being gentle and easy will get the job done.

Love gets the job done … even if it takes a little extra faith in yourself.

Chapter 13
Let It Be Easy

Love likes ease.

Many of us have a habit of making things difficult.

Whether it's our subconscious modeling of what we saw growing up or social conditioning that gives the message – ***if we don't work hard to get the thing we want, we don't deserve it.***

Either way, these are outdated ways of thinking and being in the world. We can gracefully let them go.

Phew! Isn't that a relief!

Love wants it to be easy for you. Love wants you to reduce the effort and increase your ability to receive. Love is happy for you to relax.

In any given moment we can love ourselves more by reminding ourselves to let it be easy.

Let yourself practice now. How could you make even this moment a little easier for you? Could you get more comfortable? Could you put your feet up? Could you prop a pillow behind your head? Could you relax your shoulders?

Every moment, no matter how difficult, has within it the opportunity to love ourselves more by reminding ourselves to let it be easy … and when you can't let it be easy, see if you can let it be easi**er.**

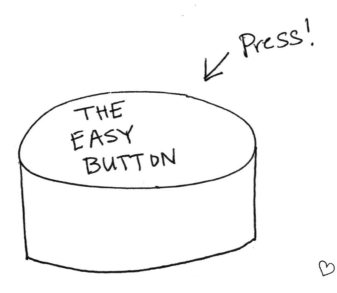

Press!

THE EASY BUTTON

Chapter 14
Celebrate Your Wins

Whatever we put our attention on, amplifies. Whatever you celebrate, you will receive more of – including the feelings associated with it.

Find something to celebrate every day, big and small. You can celebrate something you did, you received, you experienced … all of these are ways of loving yourself.

You're reading a cute little book about loving yourself more. Congratulations! Celebrate that.

You're increasing your capacity for love. Celebrate that too! Celebration is a soul-sister to gratitude.

I'm celebrating you reading this book. I'm celebrating the phenomenon that this idea about how to give yourself more love is being held in your hands right now, and through an everyday miracle, we get to connect with each other in this very moment.

Chapter 15
11 Self-Love Practices
You Can Do In 3 Minutes or Less

In a world where we often have a lot on our plate, it can help to know that adding more love need only take a few moments. Here is a list of simple self-love practices you can do any time.

Create two or three or five minutes a day to cultivate and invite more love for you. The more often you offer love to yourself, the more natural it will become … and the more love you will be able to give and receive, with less effort and more ease.

1. Read one page of a book that inspires you.

2. Walk outside and look at the sky, take a breath. Look out the window and look at a tree, take a breath.

3. Light a candle.

4. Say a prayer and add a thank you, knowing that your prayer is being answered.

5. Name three things you feel grateful for in this very moment.

I like my pillow
I like my bed
I like my curls
I like my boyfriend
I like my girlfriend
I like my chocolate
I like my cousins

I like my socks
I like my cat
I like my car
I like the sunshine
I like my eyebrows

6. Wrap your arms around yourself and say gently and sincerely, "I love myself; I deeply and completely love and accept myself."

7. Set a timer for three minutes, close your eyes and visualize yourself having the things you most desire. Really see it, feel it, receive it and enjoy it.

8. Write a short love note to yourself on a post-it and post it.

9. Set a timer and meditate for three minutes. Listen to the sounds you hear and allow your mind to rest.

10. Sing a sweet self-love song out loud to yourself. My favorite is to take part of a song I know, make up the rest and sing it to myself.

11. Put your feet up.

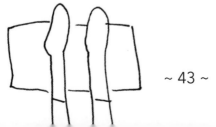

Loving yourself is both a path and a destination, an action, an idea, a feeling and a way of being. If you want others to feel loved in your presence, practice unconditionally loving yourself as if it were the most valuable thing you could do.

when I love me
It's easy for me to
Love you.

And isn't that wonderful? The love you extend to yourself always ripples out into the world, in love for others. We can change the world by loving ourselves one moment at a time. Make time to love you. It's important. You're important.

Love heals

Epilogue
A Note on Being and Doing

We are such fabulous doers. We love to do things. We love to make to-do lists and cross things off our lists. We love to get results and we love to make things happen. As long as you are enjoying doing the things, all of this is great.

Now here's a secret.

The best doings come from the best beings. What's that mean?! That means when we deliberately choose to nurture our state of being so that we feel good, whatever we do - gets done better.

When our state of being is relaxed and loving, whatever we say, gets said better.

It's our energy that people are responding to more than our actions and words.

One of the most loving things you can do for yourself is to cultivate a state of being that has you feeling good, loved, safe, cared for and caring.

Whatever the qualities you would most love to experience, you can bring into your life by bringing them into your state of being.

This is the love and magic behind loving yourself, loving your life, loving what you do and loving others.

Combine your loving, joyful energy with what you do - and ta dah! Goodness awaits.

Acknowledgments

Gratitude abounds and could fill more pages than this book. I would like to express my love and gratitude to the following people.

Thank you to Sara Connell, you were the first person I called when I knew I wanted to bring my book idea to life. I will always be grateful for your enthusiasm, guidance, support and hell- yess-ness. You are the embodiment of supporting women and their work.

To Patricia Fors, and to everyone at Muse Literary. Thank you for stewarding my book as only a talented and devoted publishing team can do. Your competence and care mean the world to me. Thank you for helping to make my dream come true.

To Jill Bernard, for writing the Cute Small Book of Improv and supporting my book idea. You are a talented genius. Go see Jill's improvised one-woman show Drum Machine, it will open your heart and thrill you.

Thank you to my mom, Carol Nathanson, for teaching me the value of being real and speaking up. Thank you for believing in me and my dreams, for loving every idea, show and project I endeavor to create. I love you.

Thank you to my dad, Larry Madorsky, you made me feel proud from the time I was a little girl. Thank you for teaching me how to throw a ball, love to win, go after my dreams and be my own boss. I love you.

Thank you to my sister, Anna, for being my sister and friend, and for knowing how to make everything fun. I love you.

To my Aunt Judie, Thank you for all the love, joy, acceptance, and belonging that anyone could wish for. You've been a light for me my whole life. You make everyone feel loved. I love you.

Thank you to my Cousin Terri, for a lifetime of love, laughter, and support. You have been the keeper of my dreams and the nurturer of my heart. I love you.

Thank you to our whole family, including Grandma Rose for our good genes and Grandpa Sam for loving me and making me laugh before I could talk.

If we travel in packs of souls, I know our family is a cluster of love, connected beyond this life and the next. I love you.

To my maternal grandmother, Connie, aka Nanny, I think about you every day. Thank you for loving me. You are with me always and I love you.

To my mentors, coaches, colleagues, and exquisite compilation of other-worldly support, Thank you for the love, growth, guidance, and encouragement. Thank for you showing me a path of exponential possibilities and miracles.

To John Patrick Morgan, our work together moved me into a new vista of love, for myself and others. Thank you for being a champion for humanity. I am your friend and cheerleader always. ♡

To Carry Peters and Stacey Morgenstern, Thank you for founding Health Coach Institute. You showed me what receiving and allowing is all about. The training and experiences I've received from you are among my favorites.

To Vanessa Broers, Thank you for being a soul-friend and coach. Your authenticity is magical. Your ability to both validate and lift others is priceless.

Thank you to Jesse Johnson for your powerful power power. I'm forever grateful for your clarity machetes and the self love you've added to my life.

To Marlo Zaber and George Bendele, you are my soul sister and soul brother. Life is a million times better with the gift of your friendship. I love you.

To my friends and family inside and out of the improv comedy world, the coaching world, the therapy world, the change-the-world-world, and beyond, the gift of your friendship is precious, and I love you.

To my husband, partner, and friend for life times, Dave, Thank you for supporting every idea and dream. Thank you for seeing me the way you do. Your love and Yes-ness have given me everything. I love you and meow you forever.

And to you, Dear Reader, to all the past, present, and future versions of you, you are worthy of the love you crave. You are more powerful than you know, and you are allowed to love yourself beyond measure. Your love and joy matter. You matter. I love you. I am you. ♡

Loving you,
Rachel

About the Author

Rachel Madorsky is a bestselling author, transformational speaker, improviser, self-love and success strategist, sought after executive coach, daughter, sister, wife, human, friend.

For more than two decades she has guided clients in creating their ideal relationships, businesses and lives. Originally from Cleveland, Ohio, Rachel lives in sunny no-more-winters Austin, Texas with her husband, where they work

with wonderful, talented people from around
the world and perform comedy pieces for their
two cats.

Rachel's mission is to help heal and uplift
the world by empowering women to give
themselves everything they ever wanted in life
now. For more information and to connect with
Rachel visit www.rachelmadorsky.com.

This magic wand is for you.
All wishes are granted!

Today is the day!